SCOOBY-DOO'S SUPER FUN BOOK

By Jo Hurley

SCHOLASTIC INC.

New York   Toronto   London   Auckland   Sydney
Mexico City   New Delhi   Hong Kong   Buenos Aires

If you purchased this book without a cover, you should be aware that this book is stolen property. It was reported as "unsold and destroyed" to the publisher, and neither the author nor the publisher has received any payment for this "stripped book."

No part of this publication may be reproduced in whole or in part, or stored in a retrieval system, or transmitted in any form or by any means, electronic, mechanical, photocopying, recording, or otherwise, without written permission of the publisher. For information regarding permission, write to Scholastic Inc., Attention: Permissions Department, 557 Broadway, New York, NY 10012.

ISBN 0-439-70864-8

Copyright © 2005 Hanna-Barbera.
SCOOBY-DOO and all related characters and elements are trademarks of and © Hanna-Barbera.
CARTOON NETWORK and logo are trademarks of and © Cartoon Network.
(s05)

Published by Scholastic Inc. All rights reserved.
SCHOLASTIC, and associated logos are trademarks and/or registered trademarks of Scholastic Inc.

Designed by Louise Bova

12 11 10 9 8 7 6 5 4 3 2 1   5 6 7 8 9/0

Printed in the U.S.A.
First printing, June 2005

Check it out! Scooby FUN on Every Page!

Table of Contents

Crisscross Puzzle: Welcome to Mystery, Inc.	7–8
Velma's Coded Message	9
Shaggy's Super Snooping Tips	10
Yuk Yuks from the Mystery Machine	11
Mini-Mystery: Sir Ghastly's Last Gulp	12
Say What? Picture Caption	13
Fill-in Mystery: The Case of the Big Stink	14–17
Monster Word Seek	19
L"OO"k Out for Sc"OO"by	20
Scooby's Favorite Knock-Knocks	21
Pup Tent Campfire Fun	22–23
Super Scrambler: Fun House Fun Time	24
Mini-Mystery: Operation Missing Sandwich	25
The Batty Bookshelf	26
The Amazing Swami Scooby	27–30
Swami Scooby's Fortune Cookie Fun	31–33
Scary Stuff Word Find	34
Say What? Picture Captions	35
Crisscross Puzzle: Alien Invaders	36
Scooby Laff Break	37
Host a Scooby Sleepover	38–40
Super Scrambler: Inside Creepy Castle	41
Phantom Phunnies	42
Mini-Mystery: Look Out! Library Ghoul!	43
Piece-of-Cake Crossword: Scooby Snackathon	44–45
Fill-in Mystery: The Case of the Swamp Thing	46–50
Scooby You! Quiz	51–55
Puzzle Answers	56–64

Rerro Everyone!

Scooby-Doo and the Mystery, Inc. gang are here with a jam-packed book of activities you can do alone—or with your friends. Wherever there's a mystery to crack or a puzzle to solve, we're ready for action . . . are you? Sharpen your pencils and break open that box of Scooby Snacks. We've got FUN to do!

♡ Shaggy
Velma
Fred
Daphne
Scooby-Dooby-Doo!

Crisscross Puzzle: Welcome to Mystery, Inc.

Think you've got what it takes to join Mystery, Inc.? Fit the words on the next page into the crisscross puzzle grid below, then we'll talk!

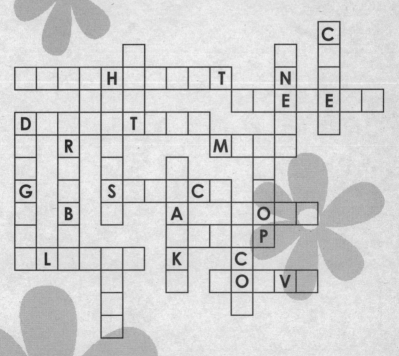

4 LETTERS
DOOR
MASK
PLOT
TRAP

5 LETTERS
CHASE
CLUES
CREEP
DECOY
SNEAK
SNOOP
SOLVE

6 LETTERS
SEARCH
SLEUTH
TRACKS

7 LETTERS
DANGERS
JEEPERS
TROUBLE

9 LETTERS
DETECTIVE

10 LETTERS
FLASHLIGHT

Answers on page 58.

Velma's Coded Message

According to my research, deciphering clues is a lot harder when they're written in CODE. On this page is the ultrasecret VELMA CODE. Can you use it to translate my secret message?

Velma Code:

A	B	C	D	E	F	G	H	I	J	K	L	M	N	O	P	Q	R	S	T	U	V	W	X	Y	Z
Z	Y	X	W	V	U	T	S	R	Q	P	O	N	M	L	K	J	I	H	G	F	E	D	C	B	A

The Message:

QRMPRVH! FMOVHH NB TOZHHVH WVXRVEV NV, GSZG'H GSV YZW TFB!

Answers on page 58.

SHAGGY'S SUPER SNOOPER TIPS

Shhhh! You sure do make a lot of noise when you turn those pages! Like, you just made as much noise as my stomach in between meals. If you want to be a sleuth like me and Scoob, you need to get quiet! Here are three super snooper tips.

Keep your eyes open. There may be footprints ahead! Nothing says "I'm a big monster on the loose and you can't catch me" better than a huge, muddy footprint. Gnomes leave little tracks like birds. Frankenstein wears a gigantic boot. Like, you have to know tracks to make tracks....

Perk up your ears. A creaky door means someone is coming. Mysterious snoring could mean a sleeping monster—and you don't want to be the one to wake it up—trust me. Footsteps? Someone is following you. You better run—F-F-FAST!

Feed your face. You'll always find half-eaten sandwiches on the mystery trail when you're snooping with Scooby and me. Like, to find the bad guys, you need to fill up on food!

WHAT'S YOUR FAVORITE SUPER SNOOPING TIP?

_____
_____
_____

YUK YUKS from the MYSTERY MACHINE!

What did the cereal say to Scooby-Doo?
Snap, crackle, PUP!

When Fred fell into the water, what was the first thing he did?
Got wet!

Why did Shaggy spend a week in a revolving door?
He was looking for the doorknob!

Why did the teeny werewolf bite Daphne's ankle?
Because he couldn't reach any higher!

What did the Scooby Snack say to Scooby?
Nothing! Scooby Snacks can't talk, silly!

How do Velma's math skills help Mystery, Inc. solve mysteries?
She knows how to add up all the clues!

What's brown and goes "Krab, krab, krab"?
Scooby-Doo barking backward!

What's brown and furry on the inside and clear on the outside?
Scooby-Doo wrapped in plastic wrap!

Scooby-Doo Mini-Mystery

SIR GHASTLY'S LAST GULP

Sir Gregory Ghastly invited the members of Mystery, Inc. to his castle for a costume party and feast. They were joined there by five other mystery guests named Slime, Moss, Shivers, Creepy, and Howl.

The mystery guests were dressed up in five different costumes: ghost, witch, ghoul, dragon, and wizard (but not in that order).

Everything was great at first. Shaggy and Scooby ate like kings. But then, in the middle of dinner, Sir Ghastly turned green and keeled over.

Someone had slipped him poison!

It was up to Scooby and the gang to figure out who did it. They had to solve the mystery with these six clues:

**The wizard arrived first and Howl arrived fourth.
Creepy arrived last.
The ghost arrived just before Creepy.
Third to arrive was the ghoul.
The witch arrived just after Slime and just before Moss.
The dragon saw the witch put poison on Sir Ghastly's plate.**

In no time, Velma made a list and had the clues sorted out. "Jinkies! I know who did it!" Velma cried.

Shaggy and Scooby knew, too. "Like, it was the witch!" Shaggy said.

So the police came and took the witch away.

DETECTIVE NOTES

Your Mini-Mystery Question:

What was the witch's name?

Answer on page 59

Say What?

What do you think Shaggy and Scooby are thinking? Fill it in.

FILL IN MYSTERY:
The Case of the Big Stink

Scooby and the gang were driving along in the Mystery Machine, when they _____ a bump in the road. "_____!" exclaimed Velma. "We almost crashed!" Daphne pointed to a _____ figure waving on the side of the road. "Hi! I'm _____. Can you help me get to _____?" _____ asked. "Ro roblem!" Scooby said. Shaggy agreed. "Like, we were just about to eat some
VERB
FUNNY SOUND
SIZE
YOUR NAME
NAME OF CITY
YOUR NAME

_____ with
HOT FOOD
_____ and
FOOD TOPPING
_____. Why
FUN DRINK
don't you join us?"

_____
YOUR NAME
climbed into the Mystery

14

Machine. Fred continued to drive on down the road. After _____ miles, Shaggy
NUMBER
started sniffing at the air. "Do you smell something?" he asked. Just then, they saw a large billboard with a picture of a _____
COLOR
_____ on it. "Look!" Daphne cried.
AMUSEMENT PARK RIDE
"A park in the middle of _____!"
PLACE
"That's _____," Fred said. All at
ADJECTIVE
once, they heard a loud scream. "W-w-w-_____!" Shaggy stuttered.
WORD THAT BEGINS WITH W
Everyone piled out of the Mystery Machine, including _____. "Let's split up
YOUR NAME
and have a look around," Velma said. She, Fred, and Daphne went one way. Scooby, Shaggy, and _____ went the
YOUR NAME
other way.

"I smell something _____," Shaggy
SMELLY WORD

15

said as they _____ into the amuse-
VERB (ENDING IN ED)

ment park. "I don't," _____
YOUR NAME

shrugged. Scooby rubbed his _____
BODY PART

and they kept walking. Suddenly, they heard a

strange humming noise. "Peeuuuuuuw!" A

_____ _____
ADJECTIVE   MONSTER

popped out from behind a wooden door.

"Peeuuuuuuw!" it cried. The trio

_____ and ran as fast as their
VERB (ENDING IN ED)

_____ could take them.
BODY PART

Unfortunately, they split up. Scooby and Shaggy

caught up with Daphne, Fred, and Velma back

at the van. "Something about this really stinks,"

Velma said. Scooby pinched his nose. "Roo

retcha!" he said.

"Is it _____ breath?" Shaggy
MONSTER

asked. "Smells more like rotten _____,"
FOOD

Daphne said. All at once, they heard the ghostly

sound again.

"Peeuuuuuuw!" The gang saw a group of

_____ float out of a rickety old
   MONSTERS

building and _____ across the park.
                ACTION VERB

They were all holding their noses. "Wait a

minute!" Velma cried. "Where's

_____?" Just then,
   YOUR NAME

_____ appeared through the door
   YOUR NAME

of the same rickety building carrying a pair of

_____ sneakers. Velma pinched her nose.
   SPORT

"I know what stinks!" she said. She pointed down

at _____'s feet. "It's your
      YOUR NAME

_____ socks!" Everyone laughed.
   PATTERN

"_____!" they cried.
   GROSS WORD

Monster Word Seek

Zoinks! Can you help Shaggy and Scooby find and circle all these words in the puzzle? Words are hidden across, down, and diagonally.

```
V E M U M M Y W B U G
A I M O O N E M I L S
M B S S M R O W B E N
P M S E E L S G E T A
I O D W I T C H A A K
R Z O W E R G O S R E
E L O O Z E A U T I D
F M W P C Y C L O P S
```

BEAST	MUMMY	WEREWOLF
BUG	OGRE	WITCH
CYCLOPS	OOZE	WOODS
DRAGON	PIRATE	WORMS
EELS	SLIME	ZOMBIE
GHOUL	SNAKE	
MOON	VAMPIRE	

Now that you have circled all the words, 5 letters remain uncircled. Place them in the blank spaces below for an answer to a monster riddle.

What kind of THING would go well with the other things in this puzzle?

A __ __ __ __ __ THING.   Answer on page 59.

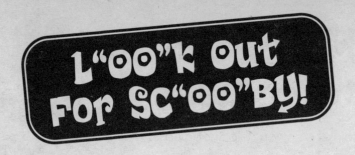

How many "OO" words can you identify? Fill in the missing letters when you've figured out the clues.

1. You'll find teachers and tests here. _C _ OO _

2. Sometimes it's full and it's always in space. __ OO __

3. Use this to get ice cream out of a carton. __ C OO __

4. Where you'll find a chimney or antenna. __ OO __

5. Dive in here and do the backstroke. __ OO __

6. Lunchtime time. __ OO __

7. I say "Cock-a-doodle doo!" __ OO __ T __ __

Extra tough one:
A wild, wet storm.

__ __ N __ OO __

Answers on page 60.

SCOOBY'S Favorite Knock-Knocks

Knock, Knock.
Who's there?
Zany!
Zany who?
Zany body seen where Daphne went?

Knock, Knock.
Who's there?
Canoe!
Canoe who?
Canoe solve a mystery as quick as Velma can?

Knock, Knock.
Who's there?
Butcher!
Butcher who?
Butcher arms around me, Scoob, I'm s-s-scared!

Knock, Knock.
Who's there?
Irish.
Irish who?
Irish I had a Scooby Snack!

Knock, Knock.
Who's there?
Luke!
Luke who?
Luke out for zombies!

Knock, Knock.
Who's there?
Howie!
Howie who?
Howie going to catch that creep?

Knock, Knock.
Who's there?
Olive!
Olive who?
Olive solving mysteries!

PUP TENT CAMPFIRE FUN!

HOWOOOOOOOOO! Last time the gang was outside camping, Fred got a few spooktacular ideas for some campfire stories — and scares. Use them when the time is "fright!"

1. When everyone is gathered around the campfire, shout "DID YOU HEAR THAT?!" at the top of your lungs. See who jumps.

2. Make a "hoo-hoo" or howling noise.

3. Make up a story. Call it "The Legend of..." whatever place you happen to be.

4. Tell the tale of the missing camper ghost. Pretend that the ghost is somewhere nearby.

5. Invent a crazy creature that might come to your campfire, like the Mega-Marshmallow Monster.

6. Make thunder and lightning sound effects.

7. Blow on a blade of grass to make a cricket

whistle or make other bug noises on your own.

8. Point up into the air at an imaginary flying saucer.

9. Get up and pretend to walk away. Then run back with a loud "BOO!" (And be sure to cackle, too. A scary laugh guarantees goose bumps.)

10. When in doubt, use the favorite story starter, "'Twas a dark and stormy night..."

Super Scrambler:
Fun House Fun Time

Unscramble the words in order and place them in the squares. When you have finished, the shaded squares will reveal the answer to the question.

1. NCOLW
2. ULGAH
3. RIMORR
4. EGMNO
5. RIPUSRES
6. SIGW
7. DREI
8. LTROL

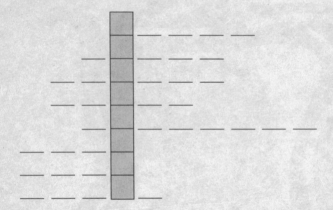

Mystery Question:

Where can you go around and around on a horse—without it moving one hoof?

Answer on page 60.

Scooby-Doo Mini-Mystery

OPERATION MISSING SANDWICH

After working on a case, Scooby and Shaggy got very, very, VERY hungry. The rest of the gang told them that a super sandwich surprise was waiting for them. But the sandwich was hidden in a locker at the bus station. Scooby and Shaggy had to find it!

Velma told them that they should go to the bus station. "The other lockers will give you a clue to where the sandwich is," Velma said. She pulled out a piece of paper with the locker numbers on it.

Lockers 6, 12, 18, 24, and ?

"Zoinks!" Shaggy exclaimed. He rubbed his tummy. "I can taste that sandwich already."

"Reah!" Scooby said. "Ret's go!"

DETECTIVE NOTES

Your Mini-Mystery Question:

What was the number of the locker where the sandwich had been hidden? (Hint: figure out the locker number by guessing what's next in the sequence of numbers.)

Answer on page 61.

The Batty Bookshelf

Welcome to Haunted Mansion
By Hugo First

Is Anyone Out There?
By I. Malone

Cooking With Scooby
By Anita Snack

There's a Ghoul in My Room!
By Olive N. Feer

Beware of Zombies
By B. Warned

Don't Open the Door
By Wade A. Minnit

THE AMAZING SWAMI SCOOBY

Rowie! A little math and the amazing Swami Scooby-Doo will tell your fortune in no time. First, write down the number of your birthday, using the month, day and year. Use the month number from the chart below.

January = 1	July = 7
February = 2	August = 8
March = 3	September = 9
April = 4	October = 10
May = 5	November = 11
June = 6	December = 12

Then, add up all the numbers in your birthdate. The year will become 4 separate numbers. For example: If your birthday is November 6, 1994, you should add up 11 + 6 + 1 + 9 + 9 + 4 = 40

You will have a two-digit number. Now, add those two numbers together.
For example: 40 is 4 + 0 = 4

This is your special number. See the next page to find out what Swami Scooby thinks about your number.

SWAMI'S GOT YOUR NUMBER!

Here's what your number could mean now and in the future . . .

1. You're a born leader who stands out from the crowd. You aren't afraid to try out for a new sports team or the school play. You're most likely to be president of the class (or the country) or on the cover of *People* magazine. Dig it!

2. Peace, man! Sometimes you are a little quiet, but you know exactly what to say when the time is right. You're the one who smoothes things out when your friends get into a fight. Got it?

3. Bring it on! You have so much energy but sometimes it's hard to get stuff done—like homework. No matter what, you know how to have a good time. For you, there's nothing better than a birthday party, sleepover, or any chance to play.

4. Jinkies! Your report card comes home with a lot of As and Bs. You don't mind working hard or getting things done. Everyone asks for your advice. You like to think big.

5. Jeepers! If you could dye your hair blue, you probably would. You don't mind taking a dare from a friend because you're fearless. You like new things, new experiences, and new ideas. That's so cool!

6. Rooowf! You are warm and caring and your friends count on you for that. (Sound like a certain Scooby?) But don't forget to be nice to yourself, too. Someday you'll make a great teacher.

7. Has anyone ever said you think too much? Well, you do, but that's a good thing. But you look at the world in a special way and everyone wishes he or she could be more like you. Someday you'll be an explorer.

8. You know how to save your allowance—and make some money. Even now you have big goals about who you want to be when you grow up. Keep it up! You have the chance to be whatever you want to be.

9. Wowie-zowie! You don't need much to inspire you. You can paint, sing, dance, and play—and you always are looking forward to the next big thing. Hang on to your dreams!

Swami Scooby's Fortune Cookie Fun

When you're busy figuring out the future, you have to have a snack. That's what Scooby and Shaggy would do. And what better treat than a fortune you can EAT?

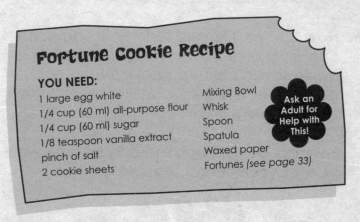

Fortune Cookie Recipe

YOU NEED:
- 1 large egg white
- 1/4 cup (60 ml) all-purpose flour
- 1/4 cup (60 ml) sugar
- 1/8 teaspoon vanilla extract
- pinch of salt
- 2 cookie sheets
- Mixing Bowl
- Whisk
- Spoon
- Spatula
- Waxed paper
- Fortunes (see page 33)

Ask an Adult for Help with This!

1. Preheat the over to 400°F (200°C). Grease two cookie sheets.

2. In a small bowl, beat the egg white and vanilla with a whisk until it gets foamy.

3. Blend flour, salt, and sugar into the egg mixture with a spoon until smooth. That's your batter.

4. Put about 6 or 8 spoonfuls of the batter onto

cookie sheets. Be sure to leave space between them. Bake for 5 minutes. The edge of each cookie should be turning golden when you take it out of the oven.

5. Use the spatula to remove the cookies and place them upside down onto waxed paper. Remember: the cookies need to be hot so you can fold them!

6. Now, put your folded fortunes inside each cookie. Then fold each cookie in half. Fold it again so the pointed edges fold toward each other. It should look like a real fortune cookie now!

7. Let the cookies cool. Share them later when you tell your friends' fortunes.

Swami Scooby's Fortune Cookie Fun

YOU NEED:
Scraps of colored paper
Pens
Scissors

Cut strips of paper 1/2 inch wide and 4 inches long.
On the paper, write down some Scooby words of wisdom, like:

Jinkies! You're a super friend.

One bark is worth a thousand words.

You always get your ghost.

May you have good luck and many snacks.

Your life is no mystery: it's great!

Don't be a zombie. Enjoy yourself.

May you find buried treasure wherever you go.

Time for another Scooby Snack!

Scary Stuff Word Find

Sometimes solving a mystery means outsmarting the monsters—and sometimes it means beating bad weather and tricky places. Can you find all the words listed below in the puzzle? Words are hidden across, down, and diagonally.

```
E T D R E D N U H T H
K E M R F A L L S Y V
A V A L A N C H E S O
U P R R D Z C A D L L
Q M S I E M Z I V B C
H A H E S D P I E E A
T W A S E A I C L A N
R S R E R C T A O B O
A N W O T T S O H G S
E L I G H T N I N G E
```

AVALANCHE
BLIZZARD
CAVE
DESERT
EARTHQUAKE
FALLS
GHOST TOWN
HOLE
LIGHTNING
MARSH
PITS
RAPIDS
SWAMP
THUNDER
VOLCANO

Answers on page 61.

Say What?

What is everyone thinking?
Fill in the thought bubbles!

Crisscross Puzzle: Alien Invaders

Fit the out-of-this-world words into the crisscross puzzle grid.

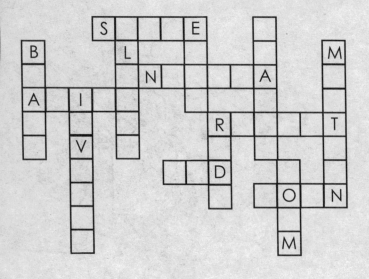

ALIEN
ANTENNA
BLAST
EYES
INVADER

MARTIAN
MOON
PLANET
POD
RIDE

ROCKET
SPACE
TRANCE
ZOOM

Answers on page 62.

Scooby Laff Break

What does Scooby munch on when he's at the movies?
Pupcorn.

What did Mystery, Inc. make for dinner with a pack of ghouls?
Spookghetti and ghoulash.

What snack did Shaggy share with a vampire?
Fangfurters.

What do Scooby and Shaggy put on their monster mashed potatoes?
Grave-y.

What do sea monsters eat for lunch?
Fish and ships.

What lunch did Shaggy share with the ghost?
His boo-logna sandwich.

HOST A SCOOBY SLEEPOVER

Wowie Zowie!

Ret's Rarty!

Good eats + groovy entertainment = a Scoob-tacular sleepover! Here are the best ways to get *your* party started.

Good Eats
Make the right party food (Scooby and Shaggy say snacks are THE most important part of every party).

Popcorn Surprise When you pop a batch of corn, serve it buttered with herbs or spices like dill, paprika, or onion powder; toss it with some grated cheese; or mix in other ingredients like peanuts, pretzels, or even banana chips

Nachos Top a plate of tortilla chips with some chunky salsa and melt cheddar cheese over the whole thing

Pizza With crazy toppings like pineapple, salami, or even chocolate chips

Miniature Sloppy Joes Make regular sloppy joe mix with ground hamburger or turkey but serve on mini-rolls

Ice Cream Cone Cakes Instead of baking cake mix in a cake pan, pour batter into flat-bottomed ice cream cones—and fill them *halfway* baking for 15 to 18 minutes

Looking for a tasty and fun snack that's good for you, too? Make a zany fruit salad, cut up vegetables and dip 'em in yogurt dip, or even put some cheese on a whole wheat cracker. Hey, Scooby and Shaggy will eat *anything!*

Groovy Games

Play detective, just like the crew from Mystery, Inc. Here are a few games you can try:

Before the party starts, plan a scavenger hunt around your house, apartment, or backyard. Make a list of items that your guests need to find. Some things on your list could be: deck of cards, toy car, baseball, copy of your favorite book, your backpack, your dog's bone, or whatever else you can think of.

Play mind reader—it's easy. Tear up a piece of paper into ten slips. Have your friends call out the names of ten animals. You pretend to write down the different names onto the slips, but really you should write down the SAME animal name on each slip. Then mix up the slips in a hat. Have one guest pull out a slip and read it. Then hold your forehead and pretend to read your friend's mind. Of course, you will guess correctly. But you need to quickly end the trick after one try so you won't be discovered.

Play ZAP. Sit in a circle and pass out all the cards from a deck to your guests. Whoever gets the Queen of Clubs is the "Zapper." That person needs to wink at each member of the circle when no one is looking. Once a person is winked at, he or she must fall out of the circle and play dead. The goal of the game is to identify the Zapper before you get zapped.

Check out a few mini-mystery books from the library and challenge your friends to a mystery or two.

Tell a group story. One person starts with a line like, "It was a dark and gloomy night." Then the next person continues the story. Go around the room and make up your own mystery.

Super Scrambler: Inside Creepy Castle

Unscramble the words below and place them in the squares. When you have finished, the shaded squares will reveal the answer to the question.

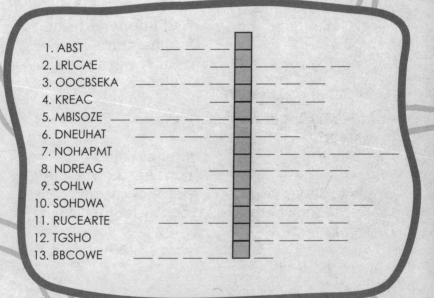

1. ABST
2. LRLCAE
3. OOCBSEKA
4. KREAC
5. MBISOZE
6. DNEUHAT
7. NOHAPMT
8. NDREAG
9. SOHLW
10. SOHDWA
11. RUCEARTE
12. TGSHO
13. BBCOWE

What is hidden behind the wall of Creepy Castle?

___ ___ ___ ___ ___

___ ___ ___ ___ ___

Answer on page 63.

PHANTOM PHUNNIES

When Shaggy meets a werewolf, what does he say?
Like, howl do you do?

What kind of stories do ghosts tell around the campfire?
People stories.

What did the zombie eat after his tooth was taken out?
The dentist!

What did Shaggy say to the Super Snowbeast?
Chill out, man.

Did you hear about Velma's *Great Mummy Mystery*?
It's all wrapped up.

How did Fred know the vampire he was chasing was sick?
It was coffin.

The Mystery, Inc. gang rides in the van, but how do ghosts get around?
A ghoul bus.

What happened when Daphne came face-to-face with the Cyclops?
It was a real eye-opener.

What did the polite monster say when he met Shaggy and Scooby for the first time?
Pleased to eat you!

Mini-Mystery

LOOK OUT! LIBRARY GHOUL!

Velma asked everyone to stop at the library. She needed to return some books she had used to research their latest mystery. Scooby, Shaggy, Fred, Daphne, and Velma each returned one of the books. The library shelved all its books in alphabetical order by title.

Scooby
Shaggy
Fred
Daphne
Velma

GREAT GHOSTS
SEA SERPENT
MONSTER MESS
GREAT GHOULS
DARKNESS FALLS

Using only the clues below, match each book with the person who returned it.

None of the people returned the books listed next to their names. For example, Velma did not return DARKNESS FALLS.
Two of the books were overdue. Shaggy carried one. The other one was called SEA SERPENT.
The books returned by Scooby and Shaggy sat next to each other on the shelf.
Fred had to pay a fine because his book was overdue.

Your Mini-Mystery Question:
Who returned each book?

Answer on page 63.

Piece-of-Cake Crossword Scooby Snackathon

Can you finish the crossword puzzle on the next page? When you have finished, seven letters appear in shaded squares. Unscramble these letters to find the word that answers the question below the puzzle.

Down

1. Cooked slices of potato with salt (or BBQ if you like)
2. These kind of beans aren't a vegetable
3. You get one with candles on your birthday
4. Shaggy likes his super-sized between two slices of bread
5. Melt cheddar over these
7. This kind of Fry doesn't really come from France
8. Short for mayonnaise
10. Sometimes this vegetable is deep-fried in rings

Across

1. Chocolate chip or oatmeal _____
3. Noise you make when you eat
6. Get it by the slice or eat a whole pie
8. In the middle of S'mores
9. Get it with butter at the movies
11. A mouse's favorite food
12. This word describes a tamale

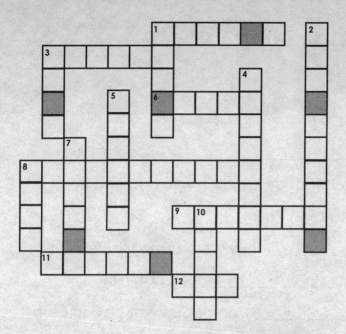

Extra-yummy question:

What snack does Scooby like chocolate-covered?

_ _ _ _ _ _ _

Answer on page 64.

Fill-in Mystery:
The Case of the Swamp Thing

"_____!" Scooby Doo
      FUNNY NOISE

howled. Shaggy joined in with a chorus from his

favorite song, The _____ of
             SNACKS

_____. They were driving to Velma's
 PLACE

cousin _____'s cabin in
          YOUR NAME

_____ Swamp. She was having prob-
 PLACE

lems. Someone wanted to buy her property but

she didn't want to sell and she needed Velma's

advice. Moments later, the van pulled into the

swamp area. Just outside the window was a

_____ as big as a
   ANIMAL

_____. "I don't like
 SOMETHING BIG

this p-p-place," Shaggy

stuttered. "Ree reither," Scooby

said. "Oh, don't worry," Velma said.

46

"Cousin _____'s place is really
         YOUR NAME

nice. You won't be scared." The Mystery

Machine drove down a _____ road
                          ADJECTIVE

a few miles more until it reached a fork in the

road. On one side of the road, stood a

_____ carrying a
KIND OF PERSON

_____. He stood next to a
   OBJECT

_____ wearing a
ANOTHER KIND OF PERSON

_____ and
ARTICLE OF CLOTHING

_____." Which way is
 KIND OF SHOES

_____'s place?" Velma
   YOUR NAME

asked the strangers. They both pointed to one

fork in the road. But before Velma and the others

could say, "Gee, _____!"
                    FUNNY WORD

one of the strangers shook his head. "Won't do

you any good driving down there," he said.

"_____ has been missing for
   YOUR NAME

_____ days." The van drove onto the
   NUMBER

house anyway. A one-_____
                         BODY PART

47

caretaker led them around the property, past

_____ trees, rows of _____
DESSERT   CANDY

bushes, and a pond filled with

_____. "Yummy!" Shaggy said. "I
FIZZY DRINK

think we should stay right here." "I think we

should take a look inside," Daphne said. Fred

and Velma agreed. "Why don't you two take a

look around the kitchen?" Fred said

to Shaggy and Scooby. Shaggy smiled. "Like,

_____!" he said. But they
FUNNY WORD

weren't so happy once they got into the

kitchen. The refrigerator was empty! "Where's

all the _____ stuff?" Shaggy asked.
        ADJECTIVE

Just then, a _____ smoke filled the
              COLOR

room. A trembling voice called out.

"_____!" Shaggy and Scooby spotted
   SCARY WORD

a _____ Swamp Creature across the
        ADJECTIVE

room. There was a trail of seaweed and

_____ on the floor. "Like, that's
  OCEAN CREATURES

one slimy dude," Shaggy said, running away. The creature tried to chase after them, but it tripped on its _____. Daphne, Fred, and
　　　　　　　　　BODY PART
Velma appeared. "Wait! That's no swamp thing!" Velma said. She leaned over and pulled off the swamp creature's _____. It was
　　　　　　　　　　　　　　　KIND OF DISGUISE
the caretaker! He had locked _____
　　　　　　　　　　　　　　　　　YOUR NAME
away in _____ while he tried to
　　　　　ROOM IN HOUSE
takeover the property. "We got you!" Velma said. "Rat's right!" Scooby said.

"_____!"
　WORD BEGIN WITH R

Scooby YOU!

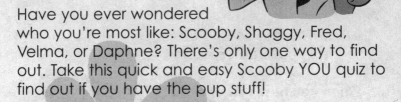

Have you ever wondered who you're most like: Scooby, Shaggy, Fred, Velma, or Daphne? There's only one way to find out. Take this quick and easy Scooby YOU quiz to find out if you have the pup stuff!

Circle the answer that applies to you. When you're done, total the number of A, B, C, D, or E answers to discover who you're like — and who's like you!

1. **You have a poster of this hanging on back of your bedroom door:**

   a) Dog Ranger, my hero!
   b) Albert Einstein, of course.
   c) Like, a surfin' dude catching a wave.
   d   The latest action flick.
   e) The pullout fashion color chart from the latest issue of *Fad* magazine.

2. **If you got a room makeover, this is what style it would be:**

   a) Pup tent.
   b) The library look.
   c) Like, beanbag chairs and fuzzy car pet. What else?
   d) Neat.
   e) Flowers and flowing curtains and purple and pink and . . .

3. **When you hear someone tell a joke, you. . .**

   a) Raff!
   b) Think about what it means.
   c) Hiccup and slap my knee, man.
   d) Laugh. Unless, of course, I don't feel like laughing.
   e) Smile sweetly and pretend like I get it.

4. **What do you and your friends like to do for fun?**

   a) Chase cars.
   b) Math problems.
   c) Like, space out.
   d) Talk about me.
   e) Look for sales at the mall.

5. **You don't leave home with out your . . .**

   a) Scooby Snacks!
   b) My spare pair of glasses.
   c) Like, what am I supposed to take?
   d) Digital organizer.
   e) Frosted pink lip gloss.

6. **What's at the bottom of your closet?**

   a) Bones and chew toys.
   b) Books, books, and more books.
   c) Half a pepperoni sandwich.
   d) My perfectly polished shoes.
   e) The greatest little miniskirt and chiffon scarf.

7. **For your next birthday, you want . . .**

   a) Yip! Yip! Yip! Super-sized Scooby Snack Pack!
   b) Subscription to *Scientific American*.
   c) Zoinks! Everything in the deli case.
   d) Customized steering wheel for the Mystery Machine.
   e) Designer duds. What else?

8. **What game do you like to play?**

   a) Retch the ball.
   b) Brain teasers are best.
   c) Eating. Like, is that a game? If not, then it's surfing. Far out!
   d) I was captain of my football team.
   e) Shop 'till I drop.

9. **What do you carry in your wallet?**

   a) A photo of Mommy Doo.
   b) My ID cards and mini-calculator.
   c) Like, who needs a wallet?
   d) License and Auto Club card.
   e) Jeepers, that's easy! Lots of cash for shopping.

Scooby You!

QUIZ KEY

If you circled mostly A's
You DO have the pup stuff! Ree-hee-hee! You and Scooby must have been separated at birth. But you have way more than Scooby Snacks in common. You are both loyal, fun-loving, and ree-lee fun!

If you circled mostly B's
According to our research, you and Velma are practically twins. Apart from reading science magazines and doing math problems for fun, you like learning new things and you know how to think on your feet. Do you say "Jinkies!" too?

If you circled mostly C's
Like, chilling out is your scene. Just like Shaggy, you hang loose with a few friends . . . and a few snacks,

of course. Bring on the double-decker hero sandwich with a super side order of slaw. Your best pal is someone who probably scored a lot of A's on this quiz. Dig it!

If you circled mostly D's
You are the boss, no doubt about that. Just like Fred, you like to make up the rules. And being a naturally born leader means you've got a bunch of friends who all look up to you. Way to go!

If you circled mostly E's
Golly! You and Daphne would make the grooviest shopping buddies. Forget following the latest trend . . . YOU are the trendsetter. You know what looks cool and how to wear it.

Answer Key

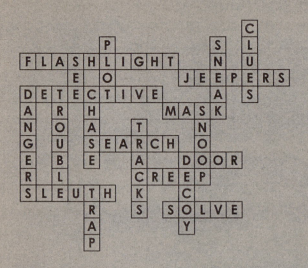

p. 7   Crisscross Puzzle: Welcome to Mystery, Inc.

p. 9   Velma's Coded Message is:

*Jinkies! Unless my glasses deceive me
. . . that's the bad guy!*

p. 12 Scooby-Doo Mini-Mystery: Sir Ghastly's Last Gulp

*The witch was **Shivers**.*

p. 19 Monster Word Seek

Answer to riddle: **Swamp.**

p. 20 L"OO"k Out for Sc"OO"by!

School
Moon
Scoop
Roof
Pool
Noon
Rooster

Extra tough one: **Monsoon**.

p. 24 Super Scrambler: Fun House Fun Time

```
      C L O W N
    L A U G H
  M I R R O R
  G N O M E
      S U R P R I S E
W I G S
R I D E
T R O L L
```

The answer to the mystery question is **carousel**.

p. 25 Mini-Mystery: Operation Missing Sandwich

The sandwich was hidden in locker 30. The first locker listed was number 6 and each one after that had the number 6 added on. So the last locker, 24, plus 6 equaled 30.

p. 34 Scary Stuff Word Find

p. 36 **Crisscross Puzzle: Alien Invaders**

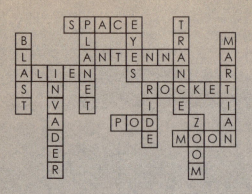

p. 41 Super Scrambler: Inside Creepy Castle

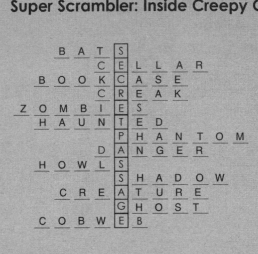

*The place is a **secret passage**.*

p. 43 Mini-Mystery: Look Out! Library Ghoul!

Scooby	GREAT GHOSTS
Shaggy	GREAT GHOULS
Fred	SEA SERPENT
Daphne	DARKNESS FALLS
Velma	MONSTER MESS

p. 44 Piece-of-Cake Crossword Scooby Snackathon

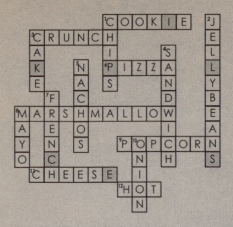

Answer to extra-yummy question: **Pickles**.